Pragmatic Wisdom Vol. 5

Stoic Principles

James Bellerjeau

A Fine Idea

Contents

Chapter One

Why Do Anything?
An Introduction to
the Stoic Lessons

D ear friends. Join me on a journey to discover what it means to live a good life. Our inspiration in this quest is Seneca's Moral Letters to Lucilius, revisited and revised for our modern times. The search for what it means to live a good life was not new in Seneca's day, and it will not be old when we are all long gone.

Although these are not Seneca's letters, they honor both his wisdom and his instructions for new students. That is, we should grapple with deep thoughts and make our understanding of the truth personal.

Because no one has a monopoly on the truth, we can each contribute to the puzzle. **The reason to do anything is to answer a question that has not been answered, or at a minimum to answer it for yourself.**

In answering life's deepest questions, would it not be foolish for us to pass by the foundational stones laid by the great thinkers who labored before us? Seneca himself in search of inspiration says in his Letter 2:

> I am wont to cross over even into the enemy's camp, — not as a deserter, but as a scout.

Let us all be avid scouts of the great thinkers, seeking out their every camp with the mindset of anthropologists unearthing meaning from among the ruins. Although Seneca's words have been mined by many for centuries, each generation keeps turning up gemstones.

Thus, with this series of Pragmatic Wisdom for Busy People, let us polish old stones to show them in a new light, and in washing off the mud and debris, reveal what fresh reflections may appear.

Be well.

PS — You can read each of the volumes independently, as it suits your time and your interests. Dedicated readers will find, however, that their understanding of each volume will increase upon reading further volumes. The sincere student may therefore wish to have the full set of Stoic letters: Pragmatic Wisdom for the Sincere Student.

Chapter Two

On Friendship and Philosophy

You are sufficient in yourself if you do not need friends for your happiness, but you need not go so far as to not want them

As I mentioned to you in a previous letter, not needing things is a way to maintain an unshakable foundation. But to say you do not need something is not to say that you will shun it if offered. So it is with friendship.

You are sufficient in yourself, and for this reason, you need no external affirmation for your happiness. But you can still desire an exchange with colleagues and interaction with the world.

Though you lose no sleep over losing all contact, that does not mean you seek isolation. You do not need millions of dollars to be happy, but that does not mean you would turn down a bonus.

My payment to you is this: You are sufficient in yourself if you do not *need* friends for your happiness, but you need not go so far as to not *want* them.

Friendship is, in any event, never far from your reach. If your desire is genuine to share, to help, to give of yourself, you will find friendship.

If, rather, you look to your friends for what they can do for you, expect the same from them. In this way, how you approach your friendships serves as a regular test of your principles.

If you are seeking friendships from any motive other than your own generosity, you may well find fortune-seekers among your fellow man. But you cannot be surprised when such friends vanish as quickly as they came if your fortunes should take a turn.

The loaded spendthrift never lacks companions, but when the flow of money ceases, only crickets remain.

Approach your friend-making with the seriousness it deserves. Is this one for whom I would sacrifice everything? If you are spurred on by noble emotions, then it is only just that you proceed. Such a friendship is worth wanting because you are not left wanting as a result of the desire.

This, my dear reader, is how we correctly understand what it means to be self-sufficient but to still want friends. Though you have everything you need within you at all times, it is natural to appreciate friends.

Mandela and McCain in their cells were left undiminished by their years of imprisonment. All they possessed was their self-possession. And having demonstrated their self-sufficiency beyond any doubt, do we doubt their joy at rejoining the company of man?

I have talked today about the value of friendship, and the difference between needing and wanting something.

To pay another installment onto my account I leave you with these insights on what is truly valuable. Scottish author Robert Louis Stevenson showed that he understood the value of friendship when he said:

A friend is a gift you give yourself.

Be well.

Chapter Three

On Like Minds

The coward looks on and says all is good; it is the hero who says your ship is veering off course. Watch carefully your instinct to reward the first one and punish the second

I am a constant cheerleader for you to be devoted to your studies, and you see me on the sidelines always urging you on. I want to see you win your self-possession because I will be the winner as a result.

This is because a friend is not always your friend, while a true friend will be true to you.

"But," you ask, "aren't you speaking in riddles?"

What most people seek out for friends, dear reader, are those who make them feel good. When such companions hold up a mirror to you, it shows no flaws, only virtues.

If in your self-reflection you see only perfection, you are not prompted to move or improve. Bad habits are left in place, and flaws are politely ignored like a fart in a crowded elevator. Let others stink in silence if this is what their friendship brings you.

Now a true friend will not flinch from the whip hand or shy away from dirty work. They do not avert their gaze from ugly truths. Having looked upon a flaw, they take the further step of exposing it to your view.

A friend who risks your ire by looking you straight in the eye is a treasure beyond price! They make themselves uncomfortable so that you may have a compass to correct your direction.

The coward looks on and says all is good; it is the hero who says your ship is veering off course. Watch carefully your instinct to reward the first one and punish the second.

I want you to be a true friend, so I get the benefit of all the lessons I have lavished upon you. Though you owe a debt to no one but yourself, for my tuition is given freely, still I wish to be the beneficiary of your progress.

How will you know if you are making progress? Here are some signs:

- if you can more easily recognize the difference between needs and wants;

- if you can feel your desire for wants diminish daily;

- if you spend more time being thankful for what you have than in distress about what you do not have;

- if you do not look externally for your satisfaction but find and nurture its source within.

When your mind is well-ordered, and we are of like minds, our efforts do not cease but rather turn to more profitable pursuits.

The learner is like a drowning swimmer, whose head only breaks the surface when pulled up by the teacher. You gasp great lungfuls of air but are soon submerged again without a helping hand.

But when you have learned to keep your head above water, both you and the teacher can safely swim to shore under your own power.

Be well.

Chapter Four

On Stoic Virtues

Today I want to talk with you about the Stoic virtues, and how to value the pursuits that people seek

T he outward appearance of a person tells you nothing of their inner value.

Consider Stephen Hawking who, though immobilized in his wheelchair, roved the limits of the universe and greatly expanded human understanding. Would you say his broken body was worth less than the perfect specimens gracing this year's fashion week?

And when their perfect figures have become disfigured from the passage of time, will you then consider them to be worth less than when they were parading down the catwalk?

Today I want to talk with you about the Stoic virtues, and how to value the pursuits that people seek. This is not only not a trivial question, dear reader, it is the only question that matters. The lack of clear answers drives people to distraction, and to seek happiness in things that can never deliver it to them.

So, what then should be a person's highest pursuit? How do they best live their lives? Let me describe what the Stoics believed.

The Stoics tried to distinguish between different types of pursuits and counted the first order as those that we should actively seek out: Joy, peace, victory, good children, the welfare of our country.

Then there are second-order conditions that we do not seek out, but which we call upon as needs arise: Bearing up well in cases of suffering and severe illness.

And finally, there are conditions about which we are indifferent, which are not in our control, including our physical stature.

The Stoics believed that virtue based upon reason, the well-ordered mind you have seen me write about so much, is the highest state a person can achieve. To control the mind and your response to circumstances is the greatest good, and this is what the wise person seeks to attain.

There is an important consequence of putting reason at the pinnacle and I would spend some time with it to make sure you follow.

The virtuous result of a well-ordered mind applying reason is the same *regardless of the circumstances*. That is, whether you are enjoying a positive pursuit in a measured way for the right reasons, or enduring a hardship for the right reasons, you are applying the same reason with the same result.

Thus, there is no difference between the Stoics' first- and second-order pursuits, even though the circumstances of the person differ greatly.

"Do you mean to say," you ask, "that there is no difference between pleasant and unpleasant things, and that we should value them equally?"

As regards virtues, dear reader, all that differs between them is the circumstances in which they are revealed. Because we regard reason as the ultimate virtue, then a hard circumstance cannot make the virtue less valuable; a joyous circumstance cannot make the virtue more valuable.

The virtue itself comes from doing things consistently, directly, and with reason. You cannot be more right than being right in your conduct, and the circumstances only change your behavior, not the reason for your behavior.

I sense you are resisting so let me make the point another way. The virtuous act is one that you do *willingly*. If you are reluctant, hesitant, afraid, or otherwise resistant, you are not behaving entirely of your own will. You will be confused, you will have doubts.

Thus, you are not behaving willingly, and your act is not the virtuous one of the well-ordered mind. When you are following reason, you will handle a beneficial tailwind or a serious hurdle in the same way, willingly.

There is of course a difference between pleasant and difficult circumstances, between joy and pain, and we are good at recognizing the differences.

Where we are able to choose, we will choose joy and avoid pain. The value in dealing virtuously with either, however, is the same. Virtue is the master of the emotions that otherwise threaten to submerge us, whether it be under waves of pleasure or waves of pain.

It is not just the external circumstance of the moment that virtue allows us to overcome. Reason also brushes off external consequence. That is, though all may criticize you, condemn you, or cast you out, the wise person does the virtuous deed all the same. The right course of action is the same regardless of the praise or blame of others that is forthcoming.

Reason also overcomes differences among individuals, as I noted above. Whether you are as rich as Jeff Bezos, or as poor as the migrants making their way across the border river with their few possessions held above the water in sacks, the virtue of your actions is not higher or lower because of your belongings.

In the same way, it does not matter whether the person is tall or short, handsome or ugly, healthy or ill. All the things that vary according to good luck and bad luck cannot affect virtue: Possessions, money, the person, their position. These all come and go, unevenly distributed and alternatively given and taken away.

Consider friendship, which is one of the things that Stoics saw as desirable. Would you value a friend more for being rich than poor, for being tall and handsome instead of short and ugly?

Would you say they are your friend so long as they hold an important position, and turn your back on them once they've left office? This would not be true friendship, because friendship looks to what is within.

Or consider one's children. What parent says they love their children differently based on their height or hair color? That because this one has the gift of gab, while the other is shy and retiring, they should be ranked in another order?

To sum up, my dear reader, virtue does not depend on circumstance, either of the person, or of the situation, including whether the act is pleasant or unpleasant.

The virtue we seek, reason and the well-ordered mind, is the same in all circumstances. Feeling joy with self-control and suffering pain with self-control are the same.

Yes, we desire the first and admire the second. To think that they are of different value, though, means you are placing value on external things and not intrinsic ones, on the clothes and not the person dressed in them.

The external things that the masses pursue provide fleeting and empty pleasure. The things that bring them anxiety are similarly just shadows, not worthy of fear.

With reason, you can master your emotions and senses. Your senses do not know what is virtuous, they merely take in what is given. Only the mind is able to recall the past, to look forward to the future, to reflect on the meaning of the moment, and ultimately the purpose of life.

It is reason that allows us to judge the good or evil of things.

The greatest good a person can possess is to conduct oneself according to what comes, in accordance with reason. Whether you are seeking out a positive pursuit or enduring a negative situation, you have equal opportunity to apply your reason.

We prefer that our bodies are strong and healthy, and that we take delight in the things we have. We would rather not suffer ill health or serious setbacks, but the value in them comes from enduring them willingly, with a calm mind.

I say if you must choose, remember that rising to a challenge can be a greater test than not letting yourself get carried away with good fortune.

Thus, we should desire to be strong in adversity even more than we should bear good fortune with equanimity.

Be well.

Chapter Five

On the Greatest Good

The greater your desired change, the larger will be the necessary expenditure of your personal resources

I taught my course on Common Law Contracts today, and because I couldn't make it to Switzerland this time, my class attended via Zoom. Do I fool myself that their faces were as eager as when they cannot hide because they are sitting in front of me in the classroom?

Though I am delivering the same message that I have many times before, are my messages as clear as when I can look into the pupils of my pupils' eyes? A conversation face-to-face gives countless imperceptible cues, and body language relays agreement, confusion, impatience, boredom, and more.

On the screen, I must have greater faith that though I cannot see my students seeing me, still they listen and hear me. I have learned to trust the power of imagination by writing these letters to you, my dear reader. I can now call you to mind as easily as if I am speaking to you directly.

I hope you will take it as a compliment then, and not as a sign that you need further instruction, when I tell you that I enroll you virtually in all my Zoom classes so that I can speak directly to you for the benefit of all the others. In return for your service, I will reward you today by discussing what is the greatest good that we can attain, and why.

If the world were an easier place for humankind, perhaps we would not need the lessons of philosophy so much. But why is it so difficult for the lessons to take hold? Just because the world is hard, does that mean the solution must be hard as well?

Fortune is fickle and scatters benefits unevenly, which means that some encounter only good luck while others seem to have only bad. If you wish to more reliably change the course of things, it seems clear that you will need to expend effort. The greater your desired change, the larger will be the necessary expenditure of your personal resources. Nature rewards us only grudgingly, after we have paid our respects by paying our dues.

We sacrifice now for the chance of future benefit. And before you bemoan that you hate the phrase "No pain, no gain," consider how much worse it would be to suffer the fate that many otherwise do: "Pain *and no gain*." Because pain is in store for us all, it is a matter of how much we will feel and not whether we will feel it.

The question, then, is how to best prepare ourselves for inevitable setbacks, disappointment, and pain. This is, I believe, the prize held out to us by philosophy, the thing that we should seek above else. It comes in the form of a well-ordered mind, living according to reason.

The Stoics called the supreme good I am describing as that which is honorable. They felt this virtue was found in true and consistent judgment about the nature of things.

While I can accept this as the core of the answer, dear reader, it does not feel complete. Do you become inert upon learning to accept that which you cannot avoid? Do you cease to desire to do anything when you have ceased to desire specific things? Are you indifferent to suffering to the extent that you do not seek out pleasure?

If we do not become uncaring, then why not, and what are the principles guiding us? For me what's missing so far from our discussion is the ultimate aim or direction of the person who is in the pursuit of mastering themselves by mastering their mind.

The Stoics gave a great deal of attention to cultivating the well-ordered mind because we are surrounded by temptations that lead us astray and fears that paralyze us. Seneca himself in describing his progress to Lucilius says:

> When will it be our privilege, after all the passions have been subdued and brought under our own control, to utter the words 'I have conquered!' Do you ask me whom I have conquered? ... greed, ambition, and the fear of death that has conquered the conquerors of the world.

The Stoics are celebrated precisely because successfully navigating their path is an achievement. The understandable response by many to the unfairness and pain of the world is to pursue pleasure and to give in to impulse. If life is hard, why shouldn't we seek enjoyment wherever and whenever we can find it? Isn't that at least better than meekly suffering whatever evils arise in the world?

You have heard my answer to this before, and I will not repeat it here, other than to simply say you have control over your reactions more than what happens externally, so focus on the former to be better prepared for anything arising in the latter.

Knowing that hardship and evil exist so abundantly in the world, humans have struggled to find meaning in life and to make meaning of their lives.

Although others have made suggestions across the ages, there is a modern-day thinker among us who in my view has found a significant piece of the puzzle. He is Canadian psychologist Jordan Peterson. Peterson has given much thought to the question of how humankind might respond to the conditions of the harsh world we find ourselves in.

I can only recommend to you his book *12 Rules For Life, An Antidote To Chaos.* No, I have not mislaid my general aversion to self-help books, but every now and then even a landfill yields up a treasure. I am not so dogmatic as to refuse to acknowledge genius in insight, even though it springs from a dubious source.

Peterson starts as the Stoics do, with instructions for us to first heal ourselves. I leave his detailed guidance to your own good study. Knowing though that we each have the capacity to make the world worse and to hurt others, he goes on to say we should make our ultimate aim the *alleviation of unnecessary pain and suffering.* He says

> Make that an axiom: to the best of my ability, I
> will act in a manner that leads to the alleviation
> of unnecessary pain and suffering.

This then can be our aim, our direction, the thing that gets us up off the couch and out the door.

While we are working to make ourselves better and insulate ourselves against the pain of life, can we not also help make the world a better place? We can do this now, even though we are not yet and may never be perfect ourselves.

I believe everyone can make a contribution in their own way. Some will heal the sick, others will protect the weak or bring certainty to the enforcement of laws. Others will provide food, care for the infirm and elderly, and invent new technologies. How many ways there are for us to ease the suffering of our fellow humans and improve the lot of humanity!

When I look across time now with this fresh thought in mind, I see that indeed others have also arrived at the same answer. To close this letter, but I trust not the thought from your contemplation, I will call upon two fellow travelers to continue to inspire us. First, and although it makes me sad to think of her fate, I am happy that Anne Frank's words live on:

> How wonderful it is that nobody need wait a
> single moment before starting to improve the
> world.

And finally, to give us comfort that we can find personal meaning in easing others' suffering, that the effort is worth the sacrifice, let us listen to the Dalai Lama when he says:

If you want others to be happy, practice compassion. If you want to be happy, practice compassion.

Be well.

Chapter Six

On the Rule of Law

The rule of law is a gift beyond price that should be defended at all costs

There is a public virtue that is as important for the modern philosopher as the private virtue I have been encouraging you to cultivate. Although we remind ourselves to place no value in external things, still we operate in the external world.

"What is this public good," you ask, "and why is it of benefit to the philosopher?" I will tell you, dear reader, so that you may give it the proper respect and through your actions also reinforce it: It is the rule of law.

We can think of the rule of law as the reason of a well-ordered mind applied to the body politic on a society-wide scale. Just as we individuals know, or rather we should know and must continually remind ourselves, that our actions have predictable consequences, so the rule of law gives us certainty that defined actions will have guaranteed results:

- If we enter into a binding contract in which I am to lease an apartment from you, then I may be sure that

I will have quiet enjoyment of it as of the agreed date for the agreed sum, or I will have a remedy that I can reliably enforce.

- Property that belongs to a person, the fruit of their personal labor, cannot be taken from them by any other person without due process of law.

- The state will protect your person from physical harm by another, and though it is more powerful than every citizen, the state will not prevent even the weakest from speaking their mind freely.

Though some of our fellow citizens accept these blessings without a thought, the philosopher knows to praise them above all else. For it is the rule of law and its governing of external things that gives us the freedom to focus on internal things.

When we know that our person and our property are secure from assault, we ourselves become the only person who can create a real threat to our happiness. When we know that we can not only think freely but talk freely, this allows us to share our learnings and let wisdom grow in any individual where it has taken root.

"But aren't the benefits of the rule of law as you've described available to all?"

Indeed, they are, at least within the same society where the rule of law is applied. But though a commodity is equally distributed, it will be prized most highly by those who have contemplated its worth.

How ironic that we only come to appreciate the worth of something after it has been taken from us.

- A sailor cast adrift will appreciate the sight of shore more heartily than those who walk the same streets daily.

- A starving man will approach the buffet with an appetite not shared by his well-fed fellow diners.

- Citizens of a country at war will relish a quiet morning uninterrupted by martial cries far more than those who have only known peace.

Wallowing in our peace and prosperity, too many have forgotten that our condition is not the default in human history, and that our riches have been hard fought for and hard won.

"Are you saying that suffering is the precondition for appreciation," you ask, "and do you suggest that philosophers are the only ones who have suffered?"

Give me a moment, my dear reader! I am about the explanation, and I need you to be a patient traveling companion as I make my way. Do not rush me through the waypoints just because you think you have sighted our ultimate destination. To travel well is to experience the journey and not just to arrive. Keep faithfully with me on the journey and I promise you will not look back and consider our stops to have been wasted time.

Here is what I mean to say when I say that one must recognize the true value of a thing to properly appreciate it. The citizens in the wealthiest and most secure countries have become so preoccupied with possessions and status that they risk losing everything of value they have gained by seeking things of little value.

Consider the Western obsession with income inequality. Many wring their hands and wail that the top 1% have more wealth than they need, when everyone in society has seen their standard of living rise above that of kings a few generations ago.

Truly we are blind when we can see only that our neighbor has a crumb more than us. We lose sight of the fact that we ourselves have mountains more than just about every other person alive today, let alone across the sweep of history.

The situation is more dire than you would at first think. When people argue that the wealthy should not be allowed to keep the harvest they have brought in, that it shall be forcibly wrested from them and redistributed, not to the needy but to the mere wanting, we are pouring powerful acid on one of the pillars of the rule of law.

This corrosive once applied inevitably spills over onto the other pillars: Their speech is offensive and serves no purpose, what harm is there in censoring it; certain persons have received power and prestige out of proportion to their numbers, shall we not redistribute positions and status more equitably?

Though they are separated by just two letters, *equity* and *equality* could not operate at more opposite ends of humankind. Because you cannot make some plants grow as high as others, the only way to create parity when seeking *equity* is to cut all down to the same size.

It is true that the condition otherwise guaranteed by the rule of law, *equality* of treatment in all things, means some will take to the conditions of the soil and thrive, while others languish. But do we tear up the entire field, plow it under and salt the earth, because some seeds are strewn on rocky ground or are shaded by their neighbors' faster growth?

I can see the scythes, pitchforks, and plows none too far, dear reader, lit up by the glow of the mobs' torches. The hunger for more is insatiable and knows no reason. It will burn and destroy what it cannot possess, for spite also knows no reason.

Thus I tell you that the rule of law is a gift beyond price that should be defended at all costs. If philosophers see the truth in this it is our duty to spread the word.

Every person who comes to see that taking things to oneself does not add to the stock of joy in the world but only adds to its misery, is one member of the mob quietly slipping away, one less building torched. It is our sacred duty to protect and preserve the rule of law so that more may become rich in internal reason.

Be well.

Chapter Seven

On Internal Versus External Value

If you take a step, even a tiny step, in the direction of your choosing, you will have improved your situation over that of yesterday

I do not chasten you, dear reader, though it seems you have taken my latest letter to this effect. Believe me when I tell you that I see in you a trusted, fellow traveler, whose eyes and ears are open and receptive.

When I become dogmatic and exhort you, it is not because I think you do not hear or are stubborn, but because I am driven to passion by the strength of the thought. I rejoice that I can share these thoughts with you, and through you, many others will hear you speak.

I have made the case that external things are not to be valued and that true value is found within. The well-ordered mind following the precepts of reason is self-sufficient, which is the only possession that is worth pursuing.

If we are to have any hope of gaining adherents, we must make this case persuasively. Just because I repeat a point does not make it true. So let me try to rephrase the argument, to reframe it so that we see its contours in a different light.

Before the average person can be convinced to look within, we must first convince them that the external things they have been taught to value are but poor facsimiles offering false promises of lasting contentment.

Let us start our proposition to our fellow travelers by asking them a few questions:

"Are you happy, my friend, are you content? Are your wants satisfied and your fears quelled?"

If our conversational partner answers "Yes, I have everything I need. I am peaceful and untroubled," then our position is no longer that of the prosecutor, but the attentive student. Let us listen to this wise person explain how they have found contentment, and probe whether it is built on a lasting base, or is the result of good Fortune alone.

In any event, I have little worry that we will spend too many hours in such pleasant conversation. The answer to our question will more frequently be a version of the following, "Well no, not yet. How could I be? I am troubled by a boss who micromanages me, a spouse who misunderstands me, and ungrateful children who do not appreciate the sacrifices I have made for them.

"And can you believe I found out my co-worker makes more than me, even though I have as much experience as he does?

Hey, did I tell you about the vacation we have planned this summer? We're renting a cottage on Cape Cod ..." And so on, you may insert your own variation of the theme.

Everywhere we go we observe that everyone we meet is beset with expectations. Expectations of how their life is supposed to go, how their career is supposed to progress, and how their material wealth and possessions are meant to grow.

They are beset by worries: That they will not meet their true love, they will not land their dream job, that they will not be rich or famous. They are plagued by fears. What if they or their loved ones fall ill, or they fall prey to identity thieves, or heaven forbid that a disgruntled soul turns to violence and they are caught in a mass shooting?

You can almost read the anxious thoughts running across their anguished faces: "A COVID mutation might carry off my parents. Ooh, what if *I* become a COVID long-hauler? Wait, is that a Boeing 737 MAX you expect me to board? Hmmm, the car is no safe haven either. Don't we have to drive through downtown, and what if we are car-jacked?" I tell you, dear reader, there is no hell to match the ones people create in their imaginations.

Having asked our hypothetical partners to describe their current state of mind, we trust that they will acknowledge when they are not satisfied. What is the next step in your conversational journey?

Well, I know from experience one potential path you may safely avoid. Waste no time telling a person that they should be happy because they have objectively more than (take your pick): A poor child in India, all of the people in Africa, the unfree inhabitants of China, the downtrodden South Americans, or indeed any or all of humanity that existed throughout history.

So long as a single person in sight of your friend's eye has a speck more than they do, their discontent is simply not to be reasoned away by logic. If we assume Jeff Bezos is watching Tesla's share price in fear of Elon Musk overtaking him as the world's wealthiest person, what hope is there of the average person being satisfied when their neighbor has more than them?

The only person you may safely compare a person to is themselves. In your conversation with them, you may first call before their mind a danger I have pointed out to you previously: Creeping expectations.

Remember the millionaires of the UBS survey who, at each level of wealth, felt that a third more money than they had at that moment would be just about enough? Never mind that the carrot is tied firmly to a stick that is always out of reach by design. Satisfaction is like social distancing in the pandemic of desire: The two conditions are never to approach within spitting distance of each other.

When you suggest that a person compare themselves to none other than themselves, you can also offer them one of the keys to the kingdom of happiness: Continuous improvement. For there is true magic in this formula.

If you take a step, even a tiny step, in the direction of your choosing, you will have improved your situation over that of yesterday. Do you want to exercise more? Simply park a few spaces further away in the lot and take the stairs instead of the elevator and you are a success for the day.

Now instead of your goal receding to the horizon the faster you pursue it, you will be stealthily advancing without arousing notice. Does it matter that you sneak in the back door so long as you have successfully invaded the building you were seeking to conquer?

With the seed of this thought planted and hopefully germinating, you can ask your interlocutor the next hypothetical question: "If you can travel a distance by taking incremental steps in the same direction, is there any reason to think you cannot apply this same method to your personal happiness?"

Gently, gently, dear reader, let us not spook the horse, though they have been docile enough this far. This is a delicate turn we are now navigating. I suggest you start incrementally yourself, a gentle nudge in the direction of letting go of past grievances.

We all carry many burdens and worries with us. It is human nature for us to pick up and hold close everything that we come into contact with, without regard to whether this hoarding helps or hinders us. Many of our burdens relate to the concerns of today and as many more to the uncertain promises of tomorrow. Could it be that we can safely give up dragging along with us the baggage of yesterday?

Most of us can readily see that there is a difference between the things we can influence and plan for versus things firmly rooted in the past. The past is beyond influence, beyond change. Is there really any benefit to turning events over again and again in our minds, like Smeagol turning the One Ring over and over in his skeletal hands?

A simple habit you can offer up for service here is the deep breath. Not to calm oneself, though it will also have that effect, but to use the breath as a gentle vehicle to carry off a troublesome memory. Breathe in deeply and on your exhale let the breath carry away a worry, a resentment, or a grudge with it.

These are ugly, heavy things in our minds, but breath can carry them away like the lightest of feathers if only we open the windows of our minds to let them out. I do not suggest trying to clean every cobweb from every corner in one sitting. Let continuous improvement be your guide here as well.

Today I will be content if I shed a single burden of the past. And if the burden is too heavy to be shed in a single breath, still you may blow a part of it away. A bit is gone today, a bit tomorrow, and soon what seemed unbearable has broken up into fragments and faded.

At this point, dear reader, you are well-advised to give your friend a break from your lessons, though I do not give you a reprieve yet from mine today. For though you are advising them to empty their head of worries, you have thus far only filled their head with exotic and exciting ideas. Let these ideas sit in quiet and calm for a while, lest you crowd them out by trying to stuff more into a vessel of limited size.

To be clear, I am not calling your friend or anyone stupid when suggesting their minds are limited. We each can comfortably consume only so much in a single setting. We must give some time for digestion lest we gorge ourselves and risk losing the whole meal as the body vomits it out entirely.

After some interval of time, you can inquire again, "How are you, my dear friend? Have you thought about what we discussed, and have you been able to relieve yourself of any past burdens?"

What happy news it will be to hear of their progress because no progress is too slight! Better a single step in a purposeful direction than a thousand miles spent in aimless wandering.

And if there is no progress that too is no harm. For it gives you a natural point to resume your conversation. For now, let me assume your words have borne fruit and there has been at least one such positive step. How do you guide your fellow traveler at this stage?

I would say that to *plan* for your future is not at all the same as to *worry* about your future. When you worry, you are turning over fears in your mind, much like you earlier turned over burdens of past problems.

How to deal with these unhelpful dwellers in our minds? I say unveil your fears, make them known to yourself, and write them down in every detail! This will shed light on what you have to deal with and, rather than making your worries worse, you will lessen their impact as follows: Looking over your list of fears, you will quickly see that there are many you can do something about, and some that you can do nothing about. Having identified which are which, you can now direct your efforts to the former and forget the latter.

"How can I forget a fear of something I am powerless to prevent?" your friend may ask. I say turn the question on its head and ask, "How can you *not* forget it, and banish it completely from your thoughts?"

In response to the puzzlement this may elicit, you must explain that it is futile to make yourself unhappy today because you may be unhappy tomorrow. It is folly to make yourself ill by thinking that you may one day fall ill. An asteroid may strike the Earth!

Do you dig a great hole and cover yourself in dirt such that the work is already done when the rock arrives from the heavens?

Most of the bother we cause ourselves when we worry about the future comes from contemplating our fears in an undifferentiated mass. When we call them out by name and rank them, we become the general directing which way they shall go. And I say march the ones we have no control over out of your sight and out of your mind.

If you wish, let your breath carry them off in a similar fashion, one at a time. Soon you are left with just the hard-core fears of your own making. This is where our instinct to plan is put to legitimate use.

Here is how you plan for conquering fears on topics that are within your control. After you have listed your fears, simply list a few things you can do to start to address them.

- If you are worried about advancing in your career, there are steps you can take. You will make these steps both more effective and more likely to come to pass by writing them out. The act of writing stimulates thinking, which generates ideas, which will give impulse to action.

- Are you worried about being lonely in love? Know that you are not alone in this worry and that for every single girl, there is a single boy similarly yearning, along with every other kind of pairing the heart yearns for. How will you find each other? You will not find a partner in your solitary worries, but in the steps you take to meet your fears by meeting others. One of those meetings will bring you face-to-face with your partner.

- Say you are worried about saving enough for retirement. Here too, there are steps you can take. You may not identify all the steps in one sitting, but that matters not. You will have changed your frame of reference from a person worried about events to one working on managing them, and this makes all the difference.

And do you know something wonderful? Tiny steps made consistently in a direction of your choosing will also carry you along in confronting your fears too. Continuous improvement is a wonder drug that cures many ills and advances many causes. Let it be your secret weapon that you flourish in all manner of human endeavors.

No doubt you will think it is a wonder that I have at last come to the end of today's letter. I hope I have not exhausted you, though I sense your stomach is bloated from the meal, for we have not exhausted the topic yet. Digest well, dear reader, that we may enjoy another meal together soon.

Be well.

.

Chapter Eight

On Generosity and Gratefulness

Though a person first does you a favor and then commits a harm, you should value the former greater than the latter

T oday I want to offer up some sayings at the start rather than waiting until the end. These are made not as installment payments on my account but as gifts freely given. You will understand why by the time you are done reading this mail, if you do not know already:

It is more blessed to give than to receive.

These words are attributed to that most generous of givers, Jesus, who ultimately gave his own life for the benefit of humankind.

Was anyone met with greater ungratefulness than Jesus Christ? (Maybe Donald Trump, if it is not blasphemous of me to suggest?) Was anyone more deliberately misunderstood? Why was his message so threatening to those in power?

I might have some thoughts on these questions at a later time, but I am inclined to begin our travels more on the worldly plane. Surely the Roman Emperor Marcus Aurelius was someone who had cause to expect his every word to be carefully attended to and understood. He controlled mighty armies and dispensed untold wealth and privilege.

But do you know what he taught himself to remember each morning, dear reader? We can look inside his mind to share in his thoughts:

> Begin each day by telling yourself: today I shall be meeting with interference, ingratitude, insolence, disloyalty, ill-will, and selfishness — all of them due to the offenders' ignorance of what is good or evil.

How wise Marcus Aurelius was and how generous.

"What," you say, "how do you see either wisdom or generosity in this mantra?"

It is doubly clear to me. In the first case, he is wise in acknowledging the world as it truly is, not as he wishes it would be, even though the real world is often frustrating, scary, and dangerous.

In the second case, and even more impressively in my view, Marcus Aurelius imputes no ill motive to those who would do him wrong but rather ascribes their actions to ignorance. Surely this is a deliberate act of generosity.

"But do we not fool ourselves when letting evil doers off the hook by assuming they harm us accidentally? If we are praising someone for clear seeing, do we not need to clearly see and acknowledge that the interfering, ungrateful, and selfish are sometimes acting knowingly?"

We know people act deliberately, true, but this does not mean we must assume they are acting to deliberately do us harm. They may not be aware of the impact of their words or actions. They may believe they are accomplishing a greater good, for themselves or others, in opposing us.

What Marcus Aurelius is saying is that if these persons were wise and understood the true value of things, they would not act the way they do. So even though they act deliberately, they act from ignorance.

"Now you are confusing me," you say. "Shouldn't we weigh an act of generosity against an act of evil taking into account who does it and in what circumstance? If I do my friend a favor this week, and he does not repay me, can I not acknowledge the scales are tipped out of balance?"

The way to lift the fog, my dear reader, and see things clearly when everything seems relative, is to pick the proper frame of reference. The frame of reference through which we view events is that of the well-ordered mind pursuing reason.

We are seeking first to create the conditions for satisfaction and joy within ourselves so that we may ultimately create benefits for others. We seek to alleviate unnecessary suffering, and at a minimum to not contribute to the world's stock of suffering, which is abundant enough without our adding to it.

Taking this perspective, we can discern some important lessons. Though a person first does you a favor and then commits a harm, you should value the former greater than the latter.

On the favor, we should strive to be grateful for the fact that we have received something, rather than merely valuing the thing itself. Material wants can never be satisfied by acquiring more material things. Greediness for things is the root cause of ungratefulness. No sooner have I received something than I am looking for the next thing, so do not value that which I have just been given.

If we are not to be unthinkingly ungrateful ourselves, we must properly value the generosity giving rise to the favor. We harm ourselves when we do not appreciate what we already have and that which we are given.

"But now," you ask, "what of the harm done to us by others? Even if we accept that the harm is done from ignorance, are we not still harmed?"

What, will you keep a detailed list of petty grievances like Raymond Babbitt in Rain Man, tracking every hurtful word uttered by his brother Charlie? Will we tot up the slights and insults of the day, and determine by nightfall whether we are three insults to the negative, or one compliment in plus?

An insult delivered to a wise man causes no harm. On the contrary, we welcome the input! Either our accuser is right, in which case they have done us a favor by holding up a mirror to our faults, or they are wrong, and they have only harmed themselves by uttering foolishness.

And consider this further. Do we improve our relationship with a would-be enemy by treating them as such? Do we improve their state of mind when we respond in kind to their insults? Do we try not only to keep an enemy but nurture their enmity?

The Buddha answers this correctly when he says:

> Overcome anger by peacefulness: overcome evil
> by good. Overcome the mean by generosity; and
> the man who lies by truth.

Contrast what happens when you treasure each act of kindness with the greatest gratefulness. Imagine that you forgive and forget every supposed injury that could do only psychological and not physical harm to you. Be moved by your own generous spirit to help others.

In this frame of mind, benefits will accrue to you out of proportion to what you have given to others. By being the most generous of friends, the most helpful of neighbors, and the most forgiving of debaters, you will not only disarm and win over your fiercest critics but also find favors rebounding to your benefit.

All this is but secondary because the greatest benefit is to yourself: You will be both satisfied and at peace.

Be well.

Chapter Nine

On Inspiration and Progress

Ask yourself why so many fail to make the transition from good ideas to good actions, from good thoughts to good deeds

S omewhere between inspiration and progress lies the magic that makes things happen.

"What is this magic," you ask? It is action.

We start with an idea, perhaps we have a goal we are trying to achieve. As yet we are in the realm of the mind. Well and good, for we praise the virtue of reason and a well-ordered mind above all else. But to see progress we must move from our thoughts and engage in actions.

"This is a trivial insight at best," I hear you saying.

Perhaps so for it is indeed easily said. But ask yourself why so many fail to make the transition from good ideas to good actions, from good thoughts to good deeds.

I realize I did not finish the good deed in my earlier letter describing my day to you. I left off before lunchtime even.

The addition that has most enriched my time post-full-time employment has been spending more meaningful time with my wife. We have taken up the habit of walking.

For hours we roam the paths around our house, to the extent that it makes my running seem like strolling. We have walked the treads off several pairs of shoes already, and we are eager to push our legs and our soles further.

As far and widely as we wander our conversations roam even wider: Life, love, politics; family, friends, strangers; COVID, vaccines, and healthcare; good examples, bad examples, how to moderate extremes. How to keep relationships with friends at a distance, how to support far-away family, and how best to encourage our children's development.

Ultimately all topics come back to practical questions of what to do with our time and how to live our lives. If you wonder at my appetite for philosophical conversation, dear reader, it is because I have come into the habit of daily practice with such positive reinforcement.

As enjoyable as the walks and conversations are, there comes a time when talking ends and we must implement our decisions.

People hesitate not because they lack decisiveness. It is because they fear the consequences of their decisions.

If you deliberate you are being careful and thoughtful. As soon as you act you open yourself up to criticism: Was it the right time to act, was this the right decision, did you implement it in the right way? We would rather be paralyzed and do nothing than take action and be seen to have decided wrongly.

"What will free us from deliberation purgatory and get us moving again from our paralysis of indecision," you ask?

My counsel is for you to continue talking but this time engage in some soothing self-talk. If you have applied your well-ordered thinking and are deciding for the right reasons, tell yourself that you have done well no matter the short-term outcome.

Though your plans go immediately awry, that is not the benchmark you will measure yourself against, no matter what others think or say. You will remind yourself that steady movement in a consistent direction will bring you great distances if only you are steady in your application.

Course corrections are so much easier if you are already moving, so get about the business of moving in the direction of your choosing.

That Renaissance polymath Leonardo da Vinci is said to have said as much with these words:

> I have been impressed with the urgency of doing.
> Knowing is not enough; we must apply. Being
> willing is not enough; we must do.

I would add to his wisdom an exhortation from the Buddha, who is otherwise so gentle in his expectations:

> There are only two mistakes one can make along
> the road to truth: not going all the way and not
> starting.

We must start living our lives, my dear reader, by acting them out in full measure. Otherwise, what are we waiting for?

Whether we are ready to go all the way I cannot say. But I am already walking the path of wisdom, and the further I progress the more I see. I see you clearly in my company, and I would have you continue on in this fashion.

Do you ask how to speed your own progress? I have a thought for you that you can put into action at your convenience.

I talked to you recently about the companions we have always at our sides, sharing the road with us as they inspire us with their wisdom across the ages.

To ensure you stay headed in a true direction, make it your daily habit to not only spend time with these companions but to make their wisdom your own. Synthesize the best lessons you have found as viewed through your own particular lens.

And take the final step to commit your understanding to paper, if not for the benefit of posterity, then at least to send to me. You will deepen and refine your knowledge by first seeking to mine it from within the confines of your head and then by sharing it with another.

Fear not that you are working ground well-trodden by earlier treasure hunters. There will never be a time when everything is known and all mysteries are discovered. Make your own contribution.

In this way, you will make lasting progress no matter what fruits your labors bear.

Be well.

Chapter Ten

On Doctrines (Theory)

The ultimate aim of living well is to understand the value behind our circumstances and then take deliberate actions in line with reason

Has it been deliberate on my part to keep you in a state of longing when I told you I would delay taking up the question of the importance of doctrines in philosophy? Was I trying to test your patience and give you a chance to practice your virtue in accepting situations as they are rather than as we wish them to be?

Part of the wisdom in philosophy is to know the true value of things. If you only knew what a torrent of words you would unleash by insisting on an answer, you would be more careful about asking, dear reader!

Before you start wishing that I leave off before I have begun, I will take up the question where we left off, which is whether a well-ordered mind and right reason can be brought about by precepts alone, or whether more is needed.

I hope I left you with the impression that precepts are helpful in many cases. Today I must acknowledge that precepts are not sufficient or successful in all cases.

You will recall that I spoke of the need for receptive ears and willing students. Many people are deep into their illusions about what things they should pursue because almost everything in society is pushing them in a different direction.

Though they are well-meaning, they are hardly likely to be improved by a saying alone, because it is too heavy a burden to lift, too great a height to climb.

Consider that from the moment we are thrust into the world we are surrounded by material things. Humankind's facility for drawing distinctions between things is unparalleled, and what was once a necessary survival skill has become the root of many problems.

Sharp discernment was surely helpful to early humans in navigating a dangerous and unforgiving world.

- Does that sound presage danger, or is it just the wind?

- Am I safe sleeping in this cave with a sturdy wall behind me and a warm fire at my feet, or shall I nap out under the stars?

- Do I prefer to eat this familiar plant, or will I dine on that new fungus?

Not only did we need to learn to tell good from bad in almost every setting, but the consequences of choosing wrongly had immediate and often fatal consequences. Nature provided us with the ultimate reinforcement about how we should behave regarding material things by killing us for misjudging.

What has happened since the early days? We have largely tamed nature. For most of us, the closest we will get to a dangerous animal is on our TV screens. Some pay lavish sums to be transported in jeeps on safaris so they may be exposed to wild animals in their natural habitat.

No, the only things now stalking modern humans are our desires and our fears. For when I say we have tamed nature, did you think I meant we have tamed our natures? When I said we are far from dangerous and wild animals, do you think I have forgotten that the most dangerous animals are humans and that we are most dangerous to ourselves?

Today because we are under no threat of privation but rather drowning in abundance, we draw distinctions between luxuries. We drive ourselves to distraction by pursuing a more expensive house or car, and Nature is not there to correct our faulty judgment.

We kill ourselves gradually with greed, jealousy, and all the other vices. The punishment is too far removed from our actions for us to take heed of how we have gone astray.

To be well-meaning and still commit mistakes out of ignorance is at least understandable, considering the circumstances of modern life. I say the ultimate aim of living well is to understand the value behind our circumstances and then take deliberate actions in line with reason.

Yes, taking correct actions simply as a result of following a precept is helpful, for it is better than making your life worse through mistakes. But this is still far from wisdom.

Thus, we must concern ourselves with the doctrines that underpin our philosophy if we are to move from sometimes making the right decision to knowing *why* it was the right decision. Only then do we have a hope of escaping our self-constructed prisons and being dragged back down into despair by circumstance.

Because following the reason of a well-ordered mind is the goal we seek, it matters not just what actions we take but the reason behind our actions. What judgment gave rise to the decision to act thusly?

From this perspective, we give no credit to the accidental act of goodness, and we give much greater condemnation to the knowing act of harm. In both cases your state of mind as you are choosing what to do is critical.

Consider this the first doctrine of Stoic philosophy that we would offer to lift our heavy burden from us. It is the vehicle by which we will first know and then master our own natures.

In our relations with others, the doctrine I would have you follow is to behave as if there are no others, only yourself. I am not preaching selfishness, but rather unity.

- Would you so eagerly harm another if you believed you were in fact harming yourself?

- Would you lie, cheat, or steal, if you were the victim of each of these crimes?

- In making the world a worse place by feeding envy and

resentment, are you not fouling your own habitat and making the world worse for yourself?

Now let's return to material things, which as I noted, we are confronted with at every turn. How shall we make use of them? What things shall we pursue?

We must consider each thing separately and place a value on it accordingly. You should know why you value some things more highly than others.

We should not listen to what people say about things, but consider the substance, the purpose, and the impact of both the seeking and the obtaining of things. Above all, your opinions of things should be the result of your own thinking.

You are lost if you surrender your judgment to that of the masses because they are fickle and see only the surface which is ever-changing.

I could say more, but in this case, I will concede what I suspect you are now thinking: Sometimes less is more.

My conclusion is this, dear reader. Precepts are a helpful, but not sufficient, contribution to living a good life. The doctrines of our philosophy provide the framework in which the precepts find their application.

Without the framework, there is no order, no reason behind our decisions. And since finding our reason is the purpose of the endeavor, it is necessary to pick up the theory behind the practice to properly put the precepts into practice.

Be well.

Chapter Eleven

On Counting on Chance

The external world provides the canvas on which our lives play out, but we provide both color and picture

T he only thing you can count on is that you cannot count on chance.

For once, dear reader, I have delivered to you the conclusion at the start of my missive. I take a chance that you will read further, for you can learn nothing more profound than what I have just written.

But if you decide to stay with me for a little while, perhaps I can explain why I think this and, equally important, what it means for you.

If you build your peace of mind on the foundation of your mind, then it is yours for so long as you have your wits about you.

The gifts of nature and of Fortune are not ours to command. This we know from cool intellect and hot experience. If you stake your happiness on external things, you are tying it to matters outside your control.

This does not mean that you cannot take happiness from external things, but only if your happiness does not depend on them.

Furthermore, we make errors in judgment about external things. The external world provides the canvas on which our lives play out, but we provide both color and picture.

- A foolish person determined to make themselves unhappy can sulk amidst the splendor and cry bitter tears of deprivation though they lack no material thing.

- They can take good Fortune unremarked and curse their luck for not getting more.

A wise person takes what is given and builds it into the greatest good:

- In privation they find endurance, in abundance they find moderation.

- When confronted with obstacles, they see opportunities to overcome them.

- Though the future is uncertain, they are not uncertain in their minds, for they know they will deal with all that comes.

- And bad luck is no bad thing because they have prepared themselves for worse. "Is this all I have to contend with?" they will say with a smile, "I was expecting much worse."

Left unchecked, our natures turn to worry about the unknown. But does it make any sense to make yourself unhappy now because you may be unhappy in the future?

Channel your natural uncertainty by guiding your thoughts to the *worst* that can happen, so you are ready for whatever happens. You need not disturb your peace by contemplating all the ways your luck can turn for the worse. Rather, build your confidence in your own resilience by remembering that you can endure and overcome any situation.

Your well-ordered mind cannot be taken from you against your will.

All that we value: Property, relationships, and life itself, is of a temporary nature.

- We may lose a friend or a treasured possession, but we need not lose them from memory. We enjoyed them for only moments it seems. Let us enjoy them permanently in our minds.

- We can lose what we have, but we can never lose what we have had.

Regret is the thief of appreciation, my dear reader. Protect your mind from it as carefully as you would guard your password vault!

If you doubt that you can overcome any obstacle, take comfort not only from all that you have already achieved but also from the good examples you can see around you.

- The courageous acts in the face of great danger.

- The generous gifts of time and money are given freely by others to ease the burdens of many.

- The patient teacher who never stops trying to light the spark in eager young minds.

Do you think these ordinary heroes never knew doubt? Do you think they sprang from a different stock than the rest of the human race?

The seeds of greatness are within us at all times. In fact, they are never more than a single deed away from springing into being.

For all that chance toys with us and seems to thwart our plans, it also gives us unexpected moments to rise above the ordinary.

It is our circumstances that provide us the opportunities, and it is our choice to do great things. I have no doubt that you will choose wisely when your opportunities arise.

Be well.

Chapter Twelve

On Making Plans

The fact that you may not achieve all that you plan for is reason only to be prepared for failure, not failing to plan and refusing to try

If I have asked you to remember anything, it is that we cannot control our fates. Fortune gives and Fortune takes away, from health to wealth to life itself.

Because we do not have the ability to control much that will happen to us, the Stoic philosophy is to focus on what you can control. This, we say, starts with our thoughts.

- We may not be able to control the weather, but we can use our reason to determine that we will not be downcast because it is overcast and that we will not weep bitter tears because it rains.

- Following the chain of logic to its ultimate conclusion, we will not weep at the end of our own lives or prevent fear from living our lives.

If we do not need specific conditions for happiness, dear reader, and we concede that the future is uncertain, does this same logic dictate that it is futile to plan for the future?

I could give you a hundred examples of well-laid plans gone awry, and you could give me a hundred of your own in return. Friends cut down at the peak of their powers, others deserving but never achieving success. The healthiest-seeming companion carried off at a stroke.

To put it bluntly, you could die today so why worry about tomorrow?

I think there are two reasons to be less strict than the Stoics, even though we agree with the starting proposition that only death is certain, and everything else is subject to the whims of chance.

But are we so fragile that we cannot live with uncertainty? Does the fact that tomorrow will be different from today in unpredictable ways offer up hope as much as it does despair?

Luck comes in many flavors, and good luck, great luck, and the best of luck are among those in abundant evidence. When we say that Fate can be cruel, are we being too harsh in our judgment if we do not also admit that Fate can be kind?

So yes, I do not need my luck to turn for the better to be able to live a good life, but I am open to the possibility that I will be lucky in some things.

And just as I will not permit the bad luck I am sure to receive ruin me, nor will I be undone by the favors of Fortune that come my way. I will use the same well-ordered reason to place the proper value on external things. Just as I do not fear death, I do not shun success, good luck, and prosperity.

"But you have not answered the question," you object, "and are only talking about dealing with events outside our control, whether they be good or bad."

You are right, dear reader and I appreciate your keeping me on track. The question was whether to plan for the future, knowing that it is unpredictable. I needed to lay this additional foundation for my answer, but I am now ready to continue.

You would readily concede, I think, that people can make their situations *worse* by their actions. Would you be so stingy as to refuse them the ability to make things better?

And if we can make situations both better and worse, surely there is no rationale to strive for anything but the best, is there? The fact that you may not achieve all that you plan for is reason only to be prepared for failure, not failing to plan and refusing to try.

Knowing that we can make things worse by inaction as much as by our actions, I say it is our duty to plan for the future and to do our best in all things.

Particularly when we raise our eyes from ourselves and remember that we have an influence on those around us, we should be spurred to action. Provided we have helped ourselves by coming into possession of our well-ordered minds, we can help countless others and make the world a better place.

Who has the potential to do more good in the world: The monk who shuts themselves in a cave and achieves perfect peace of mind, or the flawed but striving amateur who directs their efforts to aiding the broader society of which they are a part?

"You have convinced me on the first point," you say, "that uncertainty itself is no reason to retreat into inaction. But you said there were two reasons to be less strict than the Stoics. Have I missed the second?"

Nothing escapes your attention, though mine obviously wanders. The second reason is that we live in vastly different times than those of 2,000 years ago.

To read Seneca, Aurelius, and Plutarch is to read of unending human hardship: Torture, exile, the gladiator games, plots, murder, sickness, and suicide. And this was not the fate of just the ancients.

After the fall of Rome there followed a thousand years of darkness before the embers of enlightenment rekindled. In the middle of the 17th century, Thomas Hobbes spoke truly when he described the natural state of humankind without a political community:

> continual fear, and danger of violent death; and the life of man, solitary, poor, nasty, brutish, and short.

It was not my point to depress you here but to lift your spirits, so let me get back on track.

The condition for the great majority of people alive today could not be more different than that of our ill-treated ancestors. Most of us can expect to live much longer lives, free of disease, and free of the predations of our fellow people that plagued humanity for so long.

Am I so bold as to say we have conquered chance? Not at all, and you know me better. We are still subject to all the same whims of

Fate, but with one important difference, which is that our odds are so much better.

Here is where we must take the statistician and actuary to our sides. To be a Roman emperor was a most dangerous wish. They had a better than 60% chance of being murdered on the job. Today a person living in the U.S. has something like a 1 in 20,000 chance of being murdered in a given year.

Certainly not nothing, but better than an emperor. Reading the tea leaves by using the distributions of large numbers, our actuaries prepare life tables telling us our probability of death by age. What a wonderful and revealing table it is.

- Let's say you have reached the age of 39, which is the average age reached by the great mass of humanity across time. Today, your odds of dying in your 39th year are just 0.2%, half that if you are female.

- You can take a full two further decades before your odds of dying in a year reach double digits: at 59, your chances rise to 10%, 6% for females.

- And you can add yet another twenty years before you are facing the coin toss that Roman emperors would have gladly taken because it was an improvement on their odds: at 79, you have a 52% chance of dying that year, 38% if you are female.

Writing these figures to you, I am forced to conclude that your only legitimate modern complaint is to be born male, at least when it comes to longevity and risk of death.

Why even the centenarian has but one chance in three of dying, the same chance a Roman emperor had of surviving their reign.

No, we are not in a position to complain about our portion of life.

So, to recap the argument and conclude before I have too greatly increased the risk that you stop reading.

- We have excellent chances of living long lives. Those lives are still beset with uncertainty, but it is not the kind that our ancestors faced.

- We can do both good and harm by our actions, and the only choice following the right reason is to seek to do good.

- If we plan for the future, we may see our plans thwarted but we may also see them succeed. The greatest good can be accomplished by setting great plans.

Thus, it is our duty to plan for the future.

Be well.

Chapter Thirteen

On Thoughts and Actions

Although the external world almost certainly will judge you by the outcome of your actions, you must focus on the reasons for your actions

I have not been too busy to answer your question, dear reader. I just did not want to, at least not yet. People use the excuse of circumstances to pass off blame for their own decisions, but I will not do so.

We do not control circumstances, true, but we are in full control of how we react to circumstances. So, when someone says they are too busy to do something, this means simply that they have set different priorities.

You wonder why I was hesitant to answer you when I have been so willing to expand on every question up to now. When I feel myself shying away from a topic, I have learned it comes from one of three causes:

- either I do not understand it yet and so feel I have nothing useful to say; or

- I think I understand it, but I do not like the direction my thoughts are leading; or

- regardless of my understanding, I do not like the topic.

"What sorts of questions fall into this latter category," you ask.

They are questions the answers to which serve only to amuse and not to enlighten. In other words, the topic is a diversion, and learning about it may bring you some knowledge but will not bring you further along the path to wisdom.

In remembering that I have much to learn myself, however, I can be of a more generous spirit in this instance. Perhaps your question is one that will bring wisdom, and it is merely my own blindness that prevents me from seeing the way.

So, you have asked if the operation of the well-ordered mind, namely our thoughts, is itself equivalent to the actions we take or whether one is superior to the other.

This is not a "which came first" chicken and egg situation, but more a "can one exist without the other" situation.

- We know people can act with bad intention and so cause harm on purpose.

- And we know they can act with good intentions and create a good outcome on purpose.

- I think the more interesting category of actions comes about when people act without seemingly good or bad intentions and so appear to cause harm or good accidentally or unknowingly.

In the world of business, we tend to judge actions by their effects. If your action harmed me, then I do not need to wonder about your motivation because the important thing is I have been harmed. If a situation benefits me, I do not need to question whether it was intended to be beneficial because I still profit from it.

We have been helped or hurt, and can we identify the cause? Having identified the action, we do not spend much time guessing at the motive.

But to the extent we feel it necessary to judge motivations in business, we are comfortable to infer motives from actions. Sometimes we want to understand motives to be better prepared for future actions.

We are guided in the direction of looking at the impact of actions because antitrust laws prevent us from talking to competitors. And is it really necessary to ask a competitor if they wished to gain market share when they lowered their prices? Moreover, if we did ask them, would we be responsible businesspersons if we trusted their answer?

I am reminded of the wise words of Confucius when he said

> At first, my way of dealing with others was to listen to their words and to take their actions upon trust. Now, my way is to listen to what they say and then to watch what they do.

People lie, they mislead, and more charitably, they sometimes do not understand their motivations themselves.

Let us leave the world of business and enter the realm of law. In criminal law the question of motives is paramount. The action is given, the only question is one of intent. What was the defendant's state of mind when they committed the crime?

We treat someone who accidentally killed a person very differently from someone who did it in a fit of rage, and differently yet again if they planned the foul deed. But is the legal world really so different from that of business?

To start with, how many defendants are telling the truth when we observe almost all of them insisting they did not commit the crime? I cannot believe our police or prosecutors are so inept that they never manage to identify the responsible perpetrator even some of the time.

Can they make mistakes? Most definitely for they are only human. But it strains credulity to assume they are mistaken all of the time, every time. So, the logical conclusion is that defendants lie to protect themselves. Our system is such that we do not have to help lay out the rope for our hangman, and this is good and proper.

What is the court and jury to do? We fall back on the weight of the evidence. A case proved by circumstantial evidence is nothing more than inferring motives from actions.

The prosecution seeks to establish that the defendant took certain actions. The judge instructs the jury that they are entitled to infer the defendant took them with a specific intention. The defendant will not tell us their mind, so we read their mind by inferring their motivation from their actions.

Finally, we come to the crux of the question. We know it is possible to say one thing and mean another. Is it possible to *think* one way and *act* another?

It is possible to think an evil thought but nonetheless act another way. Every child forced to apologize to their sibling at the end of an unresolved squabble is familiar with this situation.

But how about the consequences of acting in pursuit of a virtuous thought that is the product of a well-ordered mind? Can such an act be of equal value to the reasoned thought?

"But wait," you say, "There is no guarantee that your action will achieve the intended result. Though your intentions are pure, you can still make things worse. There's a reason for the saying 'The road to hell is paved with good intentions'."

It is indisputably true that actions may not have the desired outcome. But this is the same thing as saying we do not control external circumstances. We control our thoughts, and we control our judgment of things, but we do not fully control external things.

The good Samaritan sees a person lying on the sidewalk and seeks to aid them. In their attempts to help, a blood clot is dislodged, and the person has a stroke and dies. Was the attempted aid an evil because it had a bad outcome?

I maintain that you are responsible for your thoughts first, and your actions second. You should seek to take action in a way that represents your best effort, consistent with your thoughts. So long as your judgment is reasoned, the good or bad outcome of your actions does not make your thoughts greater or less worthy.

Moreover, because your actions can go awry and lead to consequences inconsistent with your thoughts, your thoughts are necessarily superior to your actions. The philosopher having attained the wisdom of a well-ordered mind must not let the outcome of their actions undermine the foundation of their thoughts.

Thus, I tell you that although the external world almost certainly will judge you by the outcome of your actions, you must focus on the reasons for your actions, and this alone.

I have to thank you, dear reader, for insisting that I answer your question. For now, I feel I have come to understand these words of Seneca, which I will pass on as my payment in return for your unexpected favor:

> No one, I think, rates higher or is more consecrated to virtue than he who has lost his reputation for being a good man in order to keep from losing the approval of his conscience.

Be well.

Chapter Fourteen

On Your Associations

If you wish to have a better understanding of the world, spend time in the company of people who demonstrate their depth of perception and see beyond the surface of things

I gather I depressed you in my letter presenting such a scathing indictment of our institutions of higher learning. The places that once nurtured the greatest thinkers for generations are now creating pampered disgruntled anarchists.

Moreover, these fallen intellectuals are bankrupting the country as they simultaneously enrich themselves and impoverish the minds they have been paid to better. Hmmm, now I am depressing myself in summarizing this sad state of affairs.

But my aim today is not to depress you, but rather to lift your and my spirits by describing one sure way out of the darkness and back into the light.

If we assume that there is a genuine desire for learning and self-improvement, and I believe this is always the case, is there a better path for eager students to follow? There is, and I can describe it more succinctly than I did make my case against the universities: Surround yourself with wise people who want the best for you.

We are more directly influenced by our peers than we know. Rather than being inadvertently molded into the shapes that society directs us, or that our circumstances offer up by default, use this fact to your advantage.

If you wish to be a happier person, spend time in the company of happy people. If you wish to become a sportier person, get yourself to the gym, run over to the track, and make friends with the most enthusiastic amateur athletes you know.

"Why should this be so," you ask, "And how does it work?"

Take first the simple explanation, dear reader, which also serves as a good reminder that we do not need to make everything so complicated. It works because it works! Even if I don't know why, I can still take advantage of this fact if I have observed it reliably working over and over again.

But I know you are a more demanding student so I will give you two further answers. The first I would describe as active interaction or mindful presence. That is, when you are with other people you can purposefully use them as your role models.

See how this one behaves and what it gets them. You do not have to repeat their mistakes personally to learn to avoid them. My advice here is to surround yourself with role models of your choosing and study them carefully so that you learn from the best examples possible.

That excellent scholar and teacher Confucius gave the advice in this fashion:

> If I am walking with two other men, each of them
> will serve as my teacher. I will pick out the good
> points of the one and imitate them, and the bad
> points of the other and correct them in myself.

I will also call upon Confucius to give the second of my answers. This vehicle is available to everyone, mindful or not, student or not, and it is powerful because it works unthinkingly. It is of course the power of habit, or as Confucius says:

> Men's natures are alike; it is their habits that carry
> them far apart.

To reinforce this point, and to show that modern thinkers have come to a similar conclusion, here is how Naval Ravikant describes the idea:

> You are a combination of your habits and the
> people who you spend the most time with. Many
> distinctions between people who get happier as
> they get older and people who don't can be
> explained by what habits they have developed.

If you wish to have a better understanding of the world, spend time in the company of people who demonstrate their depth of perception and see beyond the surface of things.

And do not assume that I mean you must find these clear thinkers around the water cooler at work! Take into your arms a book by a great philosopher, and you will have made a worthy friend indeed. If you make it a daily habit to spend some time in thoughtful conversation with such partners, I have no doubt you will find yourself in a better frame of mind than if you just let another hour of TikTok videos scroll by.

As much as I value the company of the great thinkers across the ages, I do not counsel you to take up the habits of the hermit. Pay attention to the people you do spend time with, whether it means you linger at the water cooler with the most helpful or seek out their association in some other setting.

You are helped in the company of people who help you in *any way*, whether mentally, physically, or emotionally, on significant matters but also in small things.

"You have been telling me that the highest virtue is the reason that comes from a well-ordered mind," you say. "Having achieved reason, and knowing how to properly value everything I confront, what good does the association with other people do me? They cannot help me reason any better."

This is true, insofar as we expect two wise people to come to the same conclusion about the nature of things and the proper course of action. Even if you believe you have attained wisdom, I would counsel you to seek the company of other wise people, and I would again give you two reasons to do so.

First, I have found no one who is not helped by positive reinforcement. Even Confucius remained a student his whole life long, taking good lessons and bad lessons from those around him.

You may have found wisdom in many things but are you certain you have found it in all things? And if you are so bold as to say you have found wisdom in all things then I offer you my second reason.

It is that you have a duty to pass on your wisdom and to teach the willing students who come after you. Confucius was also a lifelong teacher, and the world is truly a better place for his example.

In my experience, the best teachers are simultaneously expert and beginner, experienced and novice, as open in dispensing wisdom as they are in receiving it from their students.

So, seek to have a dialogue with your students and don't just lecture to them. They will certainly learn from you, and you may just learn something from them that keeps you on the path to wisdom.

Be well.

Chapter Fifteen

On Clever People

You should seek to understand the deeper meaning and be aware that in the wrong hands, words can hide as much as they reveal

T he world does not lack for clever people, dear reader. What we lack are wise people. It is a bit like the wealth-happiness dilemma we were discussing recently.

"How so," you ask.

In the sense that, like wealth, cleverness is easy to display while wisdom is something you have to seek out and discover. Most people reach for the first (wealth/cleverness), because there are many paths to obtain them, and assume it will automatically deliver the second (happiness/wisdom).

I observe that many find upon having attained the first they no longer feel the urge to pursue the second with the same vigor.

So it is with the study of philosophy. You yourself have been tempted by the quickness of sayings. They are brief, witty, and undeniably contain kernels of wisdom. To memorize them and repeat them at appropriate moments makes one seem clever.

To the uninformed, a well-placed saying can even seem profound. But you might as well call your trained parrot a philosopher if you think repeating sayings makes you wise.

The purpose of finding meaning and bringing reason to your well-ordered mind is not found in words, no matter how well you string them together. Your goal is to bring your actions in line with your reasoning.

You can learn more by observing a quiet and thoughtful person than you can by listening to the most voluble of speakers. We are distracted by surface appearances because they are the first things we see. You should seek to understand the deeper meaning and be aware that in the wrong hands, words can hide as much as they reveal.

The more physicists study smaller and smaller distances, the more they learn there are worlds within the tiniest particles. Everything we see and touch with our senses appears to be just the top layer of many more dimensions, compactified away from our current ability to perceive.

I find it fascinating how many truly staggering developments in science happened as a result of one person's thinking. The mind creates and the experiment merely provides evidence to support or disprove. So it is with your own thoughts and actions.

This is not to say that you should avoid the pleasure of words, my dear reader. I too would rather read an author who knows how to write well, not least because it is at least a hint they have learned to think well.

So long as you remember that wordplay is just that, play, you will give your other studies and your other teachers the attention they deserve.

Be well.

Chapter Sixteen

On Divining Virtue

If an analogy allows us to sneak by the defenses of our untrustworthy perception, confirmation bias, and wishful thinking, then it is a most useful comrade in arms

You have probably noticed, dear reader, what a great difference a salesperson can make to the atmosphere of a store.

We can all call to mind the cashier who seems to feel that their duties are beneath them and is sullen and surly as a result. Or the floor assistant who is alternatively bored and contemptuous by turns, who considers the browsing customer an inconvenience.

These emotional black holes seem to suck the joy and energy out of a room, co-workers and customers circling around the event horizon of their superdense discontent, from which no happiness emerges.

"What does this have to do with my question," you ask. "I wanted to learn how to tell which things are good and honorable."

The starting point is easy enough, in that you should pursue that which is honorable. An honorable action will always be a good action. Through our studies, we are seeking to train our minds to use well-ordered reason to determine the right conduct for the right reasons.

We have two principal means at our disposal to determine what is honorable, and they both start with observing the world around us.

- We can draw direct conclusions from what we see, and

- We can make analogies by considering comparable situations.

Both methods have advantages and disadvantages, and to know them in more detail is to use them more adroitly.

At first glance, direct observation seems the most useful tool for the budding philosopher. If I do X, then Y happens. Observe this more than once, say ten or a hundred times, and you can be reasonably certain something is going on, even if you do not know the mechanism.

And the beauty here is that you can call upon more than your personal experience. You have the combined lives of humanity across history to serve as your laboratory.

You see now, dear reader, why we talk so often about looking to others for good and bad examples. Every situation offers an opportunity to ask, "What were the consequences of this behavior, anticipated and unanticipated?"

With so much raw data to hand, you might wonder how it is that humankind has come to no firm conclusions as to the best courses of action. How is it that so many philosophers disagree, to say nothing of the great masses who are pulled first this way, then that, by competing advice that changes with the changing of the seasons?

Alas, our problems in relying on observation are manifold.

- Firstly, humans are not great observers. One of the more reliable findings of the social sciences is that our perceptions are faulty.

- Secondly, we are not objective observers. We seek out information that conforms to our current beliefs, even when we think we are being open-minded. Thus, unless we are vigilant, we do not put ourselves in a position where we could even observe the right examples.

- And the third problem is the most damning. It is that we filter our observations through our minds, at least when it comes to human affairs.

This means different people apply different meanings to the same situation. Worse, the same person applies a different meaning to the same situation depending on how they are feeling that day.

Hence, repeated observations do not necessarily lead to firmer conclusions, because we are unreliable, biased observers, and inconsistent in our thinking.

- If one person sees a billionaire making a sizeable donation to a charitable cause, they may consider them to have committed a most honorable act.

- Another person sees the same donation and considers the source, saying "This is ill-gotten money from selling opioids that create addiction. To accept it is to give cover for the crime."

- A third cannot get past the fact that billionaires exist at all and says "Income inequality is the worst problem facing humanity. Bill Gates is giving away just enough money to avoid facing the guillotine, no more."

Because our perception is flaky, and multiple observations can yield multiple conclusions, philosophers also make use of the second tool: Analogy.

We move from the specific situation to the general, in the hopes of finding universal principles. What we lose in detail we hope to gain in broader applicability.

Also, by moving to the realm of analogy we take ourselves away from observations that individuals will disagree over and specify situations we can agree upon.

The beauty of analogy is that you don't need agreement on every observation to accept the premise that there is some principle at work.

I tell you that money doesn't buy happiness, and you point to three wealthy friends who appear happy to you. I point to studies (and I have done so not long ago) saying there is a limit to what money can do, and how little you need to accomplish it.

Still, you will have a corner of your mind reserved stubbornly for the thought "I understand and I see this could be true for others, but it doesn't apply to me."

Let Jesus say, "It is easier for a camel to go through the eye of a needle than for a rich man to enter the kingdom of God," and you may be given pause. Not to immediately change your mind but a little space within which to think about the strength of your conviction.

Analogies help us see a topic from fresh angles. The underlying insight may be the same, but sometimes we are blocked from comprehending it directly.

It is as if the castle walls are well-defended, the drawbridge pulled high, but the back entrance remains unguarded. If an analogy allows us to sneak by the defenses of our untrustworthy perception, confirmation bias, and wishful thinking, then it is a most useful comrade in arms.

When I tell you that the mind is everything and that our thinking permits honorable action in every situation, some part of you resists. You want to respond with the obvious answer that some situations are objectively worse than others.

"Why should I be as happy getting smacked in the face with a brick as I am by the tickle of a feather?"

I do not know why the human mind resists so strongly the idea that the mind is itself the cause and the solution to many of our problems. Perhaps it is the instinct to shun responsibility because to accept responsibility is to accept ownership of the consequences.

So, philosophy approaches a topic head-on, suffers a defeat, and makes a temporary retreat. We see if there is another way past the tight defenses of the faulty thinking that plagues humankind.

If I ask you to imagine the surly shopkeeper and to picture this person vividly in your mind, you are more likely to be open to the idea that a person's bad attitude can influence not just themselves but also their surroundings.

I expect you can just as easily think now of their opposite: The person who seems delighted to be where they are and to be doing what they're doing. Helpful, attentive, and happy to answer questions. Same store, same day, separated perhaps by only a single department, but this person spreads light where the other only smothers it.

Does this analogy make it easier to believe we can shape our experiences with our thoughts? And if we credit the idea as possible, what new avenues does this open up for us to explore?

Here is one way to distinguish an optimist from a pessimist that may surprise you. The optimist looks to the negative, while the pessimist looks to the positive.

"What do you mean," you ask. "Isn't this the opposite of what the terms mean?"

Not at all, and I use the example to demonstrate once again the power of the mind.

- The optimist says "It could be worse," to convince themselves of how good their current circumstances are.

- The pessimist says "It could be better," to remind themselves of all they feel they lack.

What you believe will determine what you feel, and what you feel will determine your reality.

The honorable person uses their reason to apply judgment to all the situations life creates for them. They do not rail against Nature or Fortune but apply their reason to the circumstances they find themselves in.

An honorable person would never be a surly shopkeeper. An honorable person accepts their tasks as if they were their privilege and performs them diligently and happily.

We use a variety of words to describe aspects of virtue because they are revealed in different settings: Bravery, self-restraint, prudence, and justice. They are all merely different views of the same well-ordered reason applied to judgment in varying circumstances.

Though the situations may differ, the wise person displays consistency in judgment. Apply your perception to observing and emulating the wise person and you will be exercising virtue.

Be well.

Chapter Seventeen

On Reason of the Well-Ordered Mind

The well-ordered mind following reason is filled with happiness because it is not distracted by extraneous things or burdened with wrong opinions

Public opinion has great power to wash away reason, like a dye, from the soul of man ... unless one is right well on his guard when he engages himself in things external, and is resolved to participate only in the things themselves, and not in the feelings attendant upon them.

These words come courtesy of Plutarch. I am relaxing my strictures against sayings today, dear reader.

You may rightly ask why when I have been so stern in warning you of seeking wisdom lightly. It is because you have been a diligent student and have put in the time and effort of serious study. I know now that when you read a saying from a wise person, the summary will stir up your own thoughts of the substance behind it.

You have developed your reason to such an extent that I trust you with the temptation of these sweet vices. For though I myself have to be strict in regulating pleasures, today I will only draw upon healthy sources.

Aside from Plutarch, I have a few other favorites. Here is our old friend Marcus Aurelius, talking to himself in words that we could profitably use ourselves:

> It is in your power whenever you shall choose to retire into yourself. For nowhere either with more quiet or more freedom does a man retire than into his own soul ... and I affirm that tranquility is nothing else than the good ordering of the mind.

No recitation of condensed wisdom would be complete for me without paying tribute to Seneca himself. By seeking to be true to himself and focusing on things he could control, he served as an example to countless who came after him.

Would that we become such shining examples ourselves, dear reader.

> Set yourself free for your own sake; gather and
> save your own time. While we are postponing,
> life speeds by.

We are conducting our studies for a purpose. If we have resolved not to be idle, and even in our free time to obtain some good for ourselves, then surely it is for the aim of living good lives.

Not in the future, or at some point when we will have attained a more perfect state. Right now, today and every day. We have but one life and what a shame it is to be living unhappy or, worse, to be living in a form of suspended animation.

What can bring about this state? It is the same thing that disturbs it, namely our minds.

We mistakenly place the blame on external things, but this is an illusion that we can penetrate by careful contemplation. Thus, our highest purpose is to order our minds so that we can follow reason in all things.

It is reason that distinguishes us from all other creatures. But for all that this makes us unique, we have much more in common with other creatures than differences. We are both driven by instincts, and our appetites serve to keep us alive. They are indispensable to life.

These same appetites become insatiable when they are given too free reign. That which is instilled in us to preserve us becomes the agent of our undoing if we are unable to control ourselves. Our reason is the means by which we exercise control over our instincts and our appetites.

Our desires give us the motivation to act and in acting we find meaning. Without meaning, we may as well be like animals. Our desires thus serve a critical purpose in giving our lives direction.

But our single-minded pursuits can also lead us astray. It is all too easy for us to mistake the attainment of a goal for the purpose of our actions. Living rightly is its own reward.

In contrast, for many achievement of that which they sought so desperately is its own form of punishment by bringing new troubles with it. Our reason is the means by which we keep our desires in check.

Our critics say that we take the joy out of life by mastering our appetites and our desires.

The exact opposite is true, dear reader. The well-ordered mind following reason is filled with happiness because it is not distracted by extraneous things or burdened with wrong opinions.

We do not eliminate appetites and desires but rather turn them to serve our purposes. No meal is so enjoyed as that consumed by a hungry person. It is not the composition of the food as such, but the composition of the mind, that allows for the greatest enjoyment.

So it is with all the things that we humans pursue with such avidity. We believe the thing itself will bring us satisfaction, but we are only satisfied when the mind is in the right condition.

If you sometimes felt I have given you new burdens by asking you to think and to study, you now know it was to free you of the burden of accepting what everyone else does. Never for the sake of being contrary alone, but for the sake of seeing a better way.

Some time ago I quoted the saying "a friend is a gift you give to yourself," and I feel I have been blessed by your friendship, dear reader.

In return, I tell you that the reason of a well-ordered mind is its own gift, and I sincerely wish that gift for you.

Be well.

www.ingramcontent.com/pod-product-compliance
Lightning Source LLC
Chambersburg PA
CBHW060341050426
42449CB00011B/2812